Dropship

How to Build a Massive E-Commerce Business Using Shopify, Amazon FBA, eBay and Email Marketing to Create Wealth and Passive Income Freedom

Written By

Jason Miller

COPYRIGHT © 2019 BY JASON MILLER

All rights reserved. No part of this book may be reproduced or used in any manner without written permission of the copyright owner except for the use of quotations in a book review.

Illustrations copyright © 2019 by Ralph Neyzi

Cover photography by Ralph Neyzi

First Edition: January 2019

ISBN -- (paperback)

ISBN -- (ebook)

Produced by Jason Miller

Printed in the United States of America

Table Of Contents

Prefeace

Chapter 1: Profitable Businesses for Entrepreneurs 8

Chapter 2: Dropshipping in 2019 14

Chapter 3: The Perfect Niche Research 20

Chapter 4: Finding Suppliers 27

Chapter 5: Getting Started with Shopify 36

Chapter 6: Setting up Your First Shopify Dropshipping Store 42

Chapter 7: Pricing Strategy 55

Chapter 8: Legal Matters For A Dropshipping Business 61

Chapter 9: Optimizing Your Dropshipping Website 67

Chapter 10: How to Develop Your Brand in 2019 71

Chapter 11: Email Marketing Strategies 76

Chapter 12: Facebook Advertising for Dropshipping Business 83

Chapter 13: Getting Started With Amazon FBA 89

Chapter 14: Getting Started with eBay Dropshipping 97

Chapter 15: Outsourcing for Dropshipping 108

Conclusion 117

Preface

It is no longer uncommon for people to dream of becoming an entrepreneur. Of building a business that will allow them to create a life they love and to never worry about finances. If they only had the money, they could be living that lifestyle by tomorrow.

Having **thousands of dollars** right now to invest in a new business will still not result in an overnight success, where you all of a sudden have a million dollar business. The harsh reality is that **building a business takes time** but it doesn't have to take quite as much money.

More importantly, just because you start a business does not guarantee that it will be a **success.**

Starting a business will require a certain

mindset, one that isn't just focused on profits, but one that can see the big picture. Many fail to even start acting on their dreams of owning their own business because of the misconceptions they have about entrepreneurship. Others will start but ***quickly*** give up because of misconceptions about the work that has to first be put into it. A small group excel and turn their dreams into reality. Despite only have a few hundred dollars to invest and a lack of business knowledge, they thrive. The truth is that anyone can fall into that last group of individuals and prosper.

Now, more than ever, anyone can start their own business. Advanced technology has greatly reduced the amount of money needed to begin a business, and with opportunities like Dropshipping, it has never been easier. Simply making the commitment to follow the steps necessary to start and grow your own Dropshipping business can land you into the group of entrepreneurs who succeed.

What is dropshipping?

Why isn't everyone doing it?

What is the real potential for this kind of business?

You will not only find the answers to these question but also you will find a step-by-step guideline to start your own dropshipping business with its own storefront and methods to help you quickly grow and expand this business into one that can generate a stream of passive income for you.

Chapter 1: Profitable Businesses for Entrepreneurs

An entrepreneur needs to have the **right combination** of business sense, knowledge, and mindset. While this book will cover a majority of the business sense and unveil a plethora of knowledge, mindset is more difficult to acquire. You cannot begin starting your own business while thinking you are going to create an overnight **success story**. It will take some time, and at times it may go slower than you anticipated, but with persistence and adaptability, you can build a profitable business.

Entrepreneurs possess a certain set of characteristics, some come naturally while others need to be strengthened or **better developed.**

The Entrepreneur Mindset

- **Always have customer satisfaction in mind.** The most successful business people are those who give without the expectation of anything in return. Always going above and beyond for the customers is what will ultimately grow your business.

- **Be a problem solver.** The business world is always changing and with that change, there are bound to be problems. Being able to foresee, plan, and brainstorm a solution to these problems will keep you in business.

- Always look to grow. Entrepreneurs never seem to be satisfied. They are always looking to grow and be better. This isn't just with their business but in many areas of their lives as well. The desire to constantly gain more knowledge and improve yourself will carry over to your business model.

- **Be a self-starter.** You are your own boss. Building and growing your own business from the bottom up will require a lot of discipline and action. No one is going to come along to help you unless you hire them to do so, but even the hiring is going to require you to start. Entrepreneurs don't wait for permission, the perfect time, or for someone else to tell them what they should or need to do, they just do it.

Passive Income and E-Commerce

What makes becoming an entrepreneur so attractive is the idea of being your own boss.

Many have a misconception of what this can actually entail. Successful entrepreneurs are ones that know how to create an income doing something they are passionate about that they can build into self-sufficient revenue and eventually scale down their time commitment.

Passive income tends to refer to income that you garner from a project, job or product where you do all of the work once. You create the product or service then make it available to the public and enjoy the returns. Creating a stream of passive income used to be limited. With advancements in technology and a change in how people are buying, the opportunity to create passive income can be seized by anyone willing to do the upfront work.

E-commerce businesses tend to be a go-to for those who want to build their own business. Setting up an online store and selling products is easier than ever. Unfortunately, while it may seem easy to do there are a lot of things to consider. What will you sell? Where will you keep your inventory? How will you handle shipping, packaging, and returns?

Business Ideas for 2019

The future for the entrepreneur in the coming years appears to be limitless. The top business trends will focus on app development and virtual reality technology integration. Unless you have the knowledge and understanding of these industries, as well as the investment cost, not everyone can jump right into these business ventures. Aside from that, with the ever-changing tech industry, it is hard to create an actual passive income through these avenues.

E-commerce continues to be an ideal way

for individuals to build their own business. More and more people are learning how they can take their hobbies or crafts and create an online store to begin selling their handmade items. Additionally, others are starting their own e-commerce store by finding manufacturers to make a product that they have slightly improved.

Dropshipping is an alternative to the traditional e-commerce store. Dropshipping allows you to run an online store without worrying about creating unique items, working with manufacturers, having enough space for inventory, and all the packaging ordeals. It is a business model that most people can easily begin and grow from the comforts of their own home, in their spare time, and at their own rate.

Chapter 2: Dropshipping in 2019

What is dropshipping? Dropshipping is an easy to follow business model where you set up or list products for sale online. When someone buys these products from you, you submit that order to a supplier and the supplier will ship the product directly to the customer. The process is that simple. People of all ages, background, and education levels have been able to start and succeed in dropshipping.

Dropshipping for a Passive Income Living

Why is drop shipping a profitable business? Most people's first thoughts on something that can be run so easily is that it can't actually bring in that much of a profit. The reason why this business model is so appealing is that:

- You don't need to keep actual inventory in your home or find a space to store products.

- The investment costs and overhead are very low. Unlike most start-up businesses you can set up a dropshipping business for less than a thousand dollars.

- Everything is basically done for you. You don't worry about shipping, packaging, returns, customer complaints (in most cases) or keeping a stock of inventory. When you find the right platform, a lot of the tasks are done for you.

The Future of Dropshipping

It is obvious to see why Dropshipping is an appealing entrepreneur opportunity but is it just a trend? The term may be new, but the actual business model of dropshipping started its roots as early as the '50s. While it has evolved into more of an online business model, it has been steadily gaining more traction and doesn't seem to be disappearing anytime soon. Some things to keep in mind about the present trends and the future of dropshipping:

- Highly competitive. Low start-up cost and minimal effort result in some markets being oversaturated with dropshippers. You will need to have a competitive edge to remain in business.

- Build trust. Having a clear brand will determine the success of your dropshipping business. You must attract passionate customers and go above and beyond to deliver on what you say. People aren't just going to choose your website to buy from over the leading big chain retail sites if you don't give them a good reason to.

- Ever changing. Dropshipping is always expanding because of technology updates, minimal skill sets needed, and because more people are shopping online.

Selling Platforms

The first thing to know about dropshipping is the platforms that you can begin to build your business on. While you can buy in bulk from local chain stores or distributors, there are issues in doing so. First, when you buy inventory from these locations you run into the issue of either having to store the inventory or having your customer receive products in the retailers shipping packaging, which can result in trust issues with your customers. Instead, a simpler way to get started is to find a platform to list your products on. One of the best-known platforms is Shopify. Amazon FBA, eBay and social media platforms such as a Facebook Marketplace and Instagram Store are the best ways to expand and grow your dropshipping business.

Getting Started Quick Tips

1. Start developing a concept and begin to think about your brand. What will make your business and products stand out? A successful dropshipping business isn't just one that sells a lot of products; it is one that can stand out from competitors. A strong brand identity can allow you to do just that.

2. Quick product research will help you

identify potential products that could return high profits when first setting up your shop. Use keywords to see what people are looking for and buying on bigger online retail sites like Amazon.

3. Know potential markets and products you want to supply.

4. Think about a problem you would like to solve for potential customers. If you are struggling to find the right products, then consider a common problem that people need resolved. Think about the problems you have had and what products helped you to solve them. This can lead to some everyday overlooked products that you can market as a unique solution.

Chapter 3: The Perfect Niche Research

A niche refers to the specific category of products that will you offer in your store to a specific group of people. While most niches will make you a profit, some obviously do better than others. Taking the time to thoroughly research your intended niche can make all the difference in how much of a profit you will make and when you might expect to see a drop in sales.

Why Your Niche Matters

Choosing a niche will give your dropshipping store a clear focus. This can help you become an established seller among a specific audience. Finding the right products to sell will also be made easier when you narrow down your search options. Having a clear niche will give you an idea of what social platforms you should focus your marketing on and how you can create content that will drive more traffic to your store.

Finding Your Niche

To begin finding the right niche, you want to start listing things that interest you. What are your hobbies? Where do you spend the majority of your time and money? Keep in mind that this list is just a starting point, and after doing some research you might stumble on a niche that really intrigues you.

You want to avoid niches that have strong brand loyalty. For example, it would be difficult to start selling headphones, cell phones or other electronics as these types of products tend to have a loyal customer following. Once you have eliminated niches with strong brand loyalty, you can begin narrowing down your options more by doing some market research. Research is crucial in finding a profitable niche and you'll want to search a number of sites and keep track of your results.

- Search well-established dropshipping suppliers. You will want to type in a keyword and look for a number of products in that category; more products give you a clear idea of how many options have sold in that niche. Also, look at the number of orders; higher number orders means more of that product is being sold.

- Search Google trends. Google trends can not only show you popular search terms in a niche but can also show you how the volume changes, where in the world they are searching from, and if this is a seasonal item.

- Turn to Amazon to learn what people are looking to buy. Amazon can give you a good idea of what is popular now, as well as items that are searched for frequently.

- Social media platforms are a great place to see the content being shared about specific items. Facebook and Instagram can give you a clear idea of your market as well as how popular your niche is.

Compare your list of findings. How many times do you see items or categories repeated? Are there any products that really stuck out to you? Are there categories that you can get more specific about? If you have fitness apparel repeating across your lists, are there specific products that interest you more? After all the research there should be one or two niches that pull your focus.

Questions to ask if you think you have found your niche

1. Is this something you are passionate about? Finding products that you are passionate about will allow you to better market and attract individuals to your store. Selling products that you have some passion for will also keep you motivated while growing your business.

2. How knowledgeable are you about this niche or these products? You want to have some experience or understanding of your niche, as this can help with content creation and marketing.

3. Is this a fade? You want your niche to stand the test of time, not be one that will fade out because it is trendy. The

niche you choose can have trends in it-like accessories for instance. Accessories are a long-lasting niche but a trend product would be square-shaped sunglasses. There are also seasonal trends to take into consideration. It is wise to choose a niche that includes trends within it, as these trends can bring in big profits over a short amount of time, and also includes products that are more classic or don't go out of style easily, affording you a reliable source of sales.

4. Can you visualize your business selling this product? Visualization is a powerful tool that can create excitement and clarity regarding your chosen niche. If this is the right niche for you, then you might already be thinking of how your storefront

will look, the description and images you would show, and how you would talk about this product.

Do not rush through this process if you want to truly create a sustainable business. The biggest mistake many beginners make when entering Dropshipping is not taking the time to adequately research and define their niche. Jumping into a niche without researching first can lead you to a stale market or one that is highly competitive- which can end up being a huge loss.

Chapter 4: Finding Suppliers

Once you have discovered your perfect niche, it is time to start looking for how you will get the products to buyers. Finding the right supplier for your Dropshipping store can be a challenge. The supplier you choose can and should be a crucial asset to your business, almost like a business partner in a sense. There are a number of things to consider and to be aware of when searching for a supplier.

Domestic vs. Overseas Suppliers

Technology has made it easier to find suppliers all over the world, but should you choose a supplier that lives outside of your country or stick to one closer? There are pros and cons to each option that you will want to consider.

Domestic Suppliers:

- Can often provide shorter delivery times.

- Planning, quality inspections, and inventory tracking can be less of a hassle.

- Less of a time difference to account for can result in better communication in a more timely fashion.

- Can increase your brand identity by supporting local suppliers.

- Orders placed with local supplier won't have to take into account tariffs or go through customs which lowers the cost to ship.

- Competition in your local market can be made more difficult.

- Local suppliers are often a challenge to find.

Overseas Suppliers:

- Can find products or materials that are not available where you are located.

- There are more variations and alternatives to suppliers to choose from when going overseas.

- Manufacturing costs tend to be lower.

- The management systems used are highly effective and often more sophisticated than ones domestic suppliers implement.

- Shipping times and cost are usually a great deal higher.

- Language and clear communication can be an additional barrier to overcome.

- You will have to learn about import clearances and work with customs brokers.

- Verifying the legitimacy of an overseas supplier is more of a challenge and it is not possible to check regularly for quality control.

To make the best choice you will want to look at a few options in both categories. Failing to find legitimate suppliers can create unexpected issues that you don't want to fall victim to. Dropshipping supplier directories offer you a secure place to search through hundreds of trusted and well-established suppliers and wholesale manufacturers. The best-known directories include:

- AliDropship
- SaleHoo
- Alibaba
- Oberlo
- Worldwide Brands

If searching through a directory seems too daunting, then you can just as easily contact the manufacturer of the products you want to obtain. You can ask these manufacturers for their list of wholesale distributors. This can be a fast way to find and set up an account with the leading wholesalers in your niche.

What to Consider When Choosing a Supplier

1. Do they offer pre-pay options? Some suppliers you come across will require a minimum order amount for your first order. Often this order amount can be much higher than your average order size. Instead of ordering the minimum for one product order, you can ask if the supplier will use your pre-order amount as a credit. This can allow you to still pay the minimum amount requested but will allow you to then apply that amount to any of your dropshipping orders.

2. Do they offer international shipping? If you plan to offer your products to a worldwide audience, then you want to ensure that your supplier will actually be able and willing to ship to all parts of the world. Also, ask about their shipping time frame.

3. Technology and advanced tools. The most common problem between dropshippers and suppliers are glitches or systems failures. You want to know how the supplier handles orders, invoices, returns and additional details that can severely impact the growth and success of your business. Suppliers that are up to date with new technology and utilize innovative tools to keep things organized, are suppliers you want to strongly consider working with.

Building a Relationship

You want to ensure you have a good relationship with your supplier. The first things you should do when considering a supplier is to call them or see them face to face if possible. This will not only give you a better idea of their customer service skills, but it can give you a better sense as to whether or not this is the supplier that will fit your brand. Most often you will be assigned a representative from the supplier, which is the person you will be in contact with most frequently. This is the person you always want to maintain a friendly yet professional relationship with. Get to know how they like to work and you will be able to better work together.

Often suppliers are not going to make much time for someone just starting out in dropshipping, primarily because they see so many individuals come and go quickly. They want to know that you have long term goals. Building a relationship with your supplier that includes them in these long terms goals, is a way you can strengthen this relationship.

What to Avoid

- Insufficiently researching your supplier. There are a number of suppliers that market themselves as dropship suppliers, but in reality, they are retail stores only claiming to be wholesale suppliers. They actually mark up their prices significantly.

- Agreeing to an ongoing fee that is not through a supplier directory. Supplier directories will have a one-time fee for viewing a list of legitimate dropship suppliers. These directories thoroughly screen the suppliers and products. Direct suppliers will not ask for a monthly subscription or service fee.

- Making the process too complicated. One of the easiest ways to find reliable suppliers is to set up your dropshipping store on a dropshipping platform, like Shopify.

Chapter 5: Getting Started with Shopify

Shopify offers users the ability to set up a website and start their own e-commerce business. Those wishing to start their own dropshipping business can sign up for an account for a low monthly fee and begin listing items to sell. You are provided with a number of options to customize your shop and manage all the tasks needed in one place. Hundreds of thousands of people have set up shop and generated a significant income because of these benefits and ease of use.

Why Use Shopify

Shopify is a one-stop shop that allows you to create your own online storefront. The site takes care of ensuring that business owners have everything they need in one place to build a successful online store. You can easily create a storefront, set up payment options, find products and suppliers, as well as track shipments and marketing options.

- Integration is made easy, allowing you to set up business across other selling platforms. Knowing how you will grow your business should be one of the topics you have already carefully considered. You can start on Shopify, gain an understanding of how to run your business, and then expand your store to your blogs, social media, and even other popular online retail sites.

- Management tools provided make building your business less daunting. With built-in tools already available just about anybody can monitor their store and generate reports. Aside from the built-in tools available,

Shopify offers various apps to use with your store to better meet the needs of your business.

- Find suppliers that are legitimate and established. The process of finding a supplier can take some time, but Shopify allows you to browse products and suppliers to work with.

- The free trial period allows you to learn all the tools and customize your storefront before you commit to a plan.

What You Need to Get Started

Think of your shop name. You will want a unique and memorable name for your shop. This is where it will help to know your niche. You can come up with something catchy that individuals in your target market will relate to.

Think of what items you might want to sell. This step should already be covered as you should have a clear idea of the products you want to include in your store. Browse through Shopify's product list to see if something catches your attention to include as well.

Setting Up Your Shopify Account

Start a free trial to get familiar with your Shopify store. You just need to know your unique business name, otherwise, Shopify will require you to choose another one, and have a valid email address. After filling in your basic information you'll be asked a short series of questions in regards to what you will sell. You don't need to know exactly what you want to sell as there is an option for 'just trying' or 'not sure what to sell' in the applicable drop-down menus. You can select that you are just playing around in order to better understand how you want your storefront to look.

Learn about the different pricing plans and which is the best-suited for your business. You can always upgrade to a different plan, but know what features each offer. You can also pay for these plans on an annual or biannual basis, with an additional discount, instead of a monthly payment option. Some features to keep an eye on include:

- Professional reporting
- Reporting tools
- Gift card offers
- Staff accounts

Once you have your basic setup completed, you are ready to truly customize your storefront, add products and set up payment options. After all the research and work you've put in so far, this should be the more exciting and enjoyable part, as you will begin to see the vision you have for your store become reality.

Chapter 6: Setting up Your First Shopify Dropshipping Store

If designing your own website is the main reason you have been avoiding starting an online business, you are not alone. Properly designing a storefront for success often takes a clear understanding of layout, coding, and design. Shopify makes the process painless and incredibly easy. You can create a professional-looking website to start your business without having to know any coding or web design techniques.

Designing Your Store

Store themes

You will have a variety of themes or layouts to choose from in the theme store. Many are free and some require a small fee. Each theme allows you to view the modifications available. You can search through themes using different filters such as by industry, features, price, most recent and popularity. If you are concerned about going with a more popular theme and looking like every other storefront, keep in mind that there are many ways you can customize the layout to make it stand out.

Preview the theme you are considering by viewing the sample image. Here you will be given information on whether it is mobile-ready as well as read reviews from those who have used the theme previously. You can also view a demo of the theme by finding the green button that allows you to get a feel for the functionality. Here you can also demo the different styles that theme offers.

Once you have found your theme click the

Publish button and confirm this as the theme you want to install. You can always change your theme if you find this one doesn't suit your business needs. Now you can begin to make edits to your theme.

Steps to Edit your Theme:

1. Select your theme in your administrative screen. The theme currently installed will display at the top of your screen.

2. Make basic changes by clicking on the three dots located at the top right of your current theme box.

3. Make a duplicate of your theme which will allow you to delete changes made that you later decide you don't like.

4. Click on the Customize Theme

button located by the basic changes button. A new page should appear that shows the functionality of your store theme.

Test out all the features and explore the settings to learn what your store is capable of doing. Most themes will allow you to upload a logo, use slides, control how many items will show on the collection pages as well as colors and fonts. Some themes will also let you rearrange how the elements on your page display so you can change where your product images show up and add social buttons.

Customize Navigation

Products

Once you have the cosmetics done to your storefront, it is time to start adding your products. You can begin to do this by selecting the products tab on the navigation bar and clicking on the Add Product tab. Here you will want to be as descriptive as possible when adding the details of your product. You want to give visitors as much information as possible. You will also want to add pictures of your products and arrange them in the most visually appealing way. Be sure to include clear images of what makes your product unique such as special features. To keep your store looking clean, all pictures should be of the same size. Once you are done, save your product by clicking the button at the top right corner.

Arranging your products

You can create collections or groups to list your products and make it easy for visitors to find what they are looking for. These can be created a number of ways such as:

- Items that are for specific audiences like men or women
- Similar types of items such as rugs or wall décor
- Products you have on sale
- By size or color
- Seasonal items

Products don't have to fit into just one collection; they can appear in multiple ones. These collects are shown on your homepage to make it easier to navigate your store. You can add new items to a collection in two ways:

- Manual collections allow you to add and remove items individually.
- Automatic collections allow you to

set up criteria that products need to meet to be automatically added to that collection.

Dropshipping Apps

As you are creating your store and adding products, you might find that you would like to have additional features to either help you run your store more efficiently or to improve your customer's experience. The Shopify App Store offers a wide range of apps you can add to your store for free or a small fee. Some apps to consider:

Oberlo

One of the first apps you should add is Oberlo. This app allows you to search for products to sell and find suppliers. All shipping and product fulfillment is done through Oberlo.

Product Reviews

Having customer reviews displayed can be crucial for increasing sales and driving more traffic to your store. With this app, you give customers the option to leave a review and feedback on your products.

Push Owl

Many people may visit your store, start to build up their shopping cart, and then unexpectedly leave. This app sets automated notifications to those who have abandoned their cart, which often results in converting the sale and re-engaging visitors.

Rewards and Referrals by Swell

This app will allow you to set up reward

promotions for loyal customer and customer referrals.

Compass

Compass makes keeping track of your business metrics easy and in one place. With this app, you can quickly view data, compare how you are performing against competitors and receive recommendations for how your store could be improved.

Payment, Shipping, and Taxing

Payments

Aside from the most popular payment gateways, Shopify supports over a hundred additional payment gateways. Keep in mind that each gateway will add transaction fees and not include additional processing fees that you will also see when accepting certain credit cards.

The Shopify payment option waves transaction fees outside of those associated with credit card payment. This payment gateway, however, allows you to accept multiple currencies. Currencies are automatically converted and adjusted based on where the customer is located. Shopify payment tends to be to most favorable, especially among those just getting started because it can be cheaper and easier to implement.

Shipping

Shopify will calculate shipping rates for you but you need to define the rules yourself. From your administration page click on the shopping page and click shipping rates. Here you will be able to set weight-based rates and make adjustments based on your specific product.

Taxes

Setting up sales taxes and understanding what you need to tax can be complicated. Shopify allows you to automatically set up sales tax calculation for the products in your store. You still need to keep track of all the sales tax collected in order to report to federal and local authorities. To better understand and ensure that you are properly adding taxes to your storefront, you will want to discuss what you need to specifically do with a local tax accountant.

Adding a Domain Name

Before you can publish your page to go live, you will need to have a domain name. You can do this by buying one from Shopify and have it added automatically to your store or you can purchase a domain name from a third party and add it manually to your store. You'll need to add on an additional $10-$15 dollars a year to your business costs in either case. To add a third-party purchased domain name, click on the Setting option from the navigation section in your Shopify administration page. You will see a tab to 'Add an Existing Domain Name'. You have the option to add more than one domain name, which allows you to redirect more traffic to your Shopify storefront.

If designing your own store still frightens you, Shopify does give you the option to hire one of their Shopify website pros to build your site for you. For those who have absolutely zero computer skills and a little extra cash, this could be a wise investment to ensure your store includes all the features you need.

Chapter 7: Pricing Strategy

There is no one size fits all when it comes to properly pricing your products. While every dropshipping business succeeds on carefully pricing to have a slight edge over competitors, there are a number of strategies to consider. Since you will have products that can range from five to five hundred dollars in your store, what can be a good strategy for the higher-priced items might not work for lower-priced items. You want to ensure that you are not only covering costs, but making a profit on every product you sell.

Types of Pricing Strategies

At first glance pricing strategies may seem complex to understand, but as you use them you will become more comfortable with which one works best. The simplest pricing strategy is to take the price you are selling your product at and subtract the price you pay for that product. The price paid will include all fees associated with this product. What you are left with is the profit. Unfortunately, this straightforward method doesn't work for all products.

Fixed Markup on Cost strategy

With FMOC you add a pre-set dollar or percentage amount to all your products. For example, you have an item that sells at $10, $30, $200. Adding a 10% profit margin to each of these items would bring your selling prices to $11, $33, and $220. If you added a fixed dollar amount of $3 your selling price will change to $13, $33, $203. You'll have to consider if it would be best to add more to the lower-priced items or the higher-priced items.

Tiered Markup on Cost Strategy

Here you set a percentage to be added to products based on their cost. Items sold at $20 or under you can add a 50% markup on. Items sold between $100 and $300 might only get a 10-15% markup. This makes it easier for you to markup your lower-priced items at a higher percentage which can make them more profitable for you.

Manufacturer Suggested Retail Price Strategy

The MSRP method can be ideal when you are just beginning in dropshipping. Vendors will often supply you with the suggested retail price for the products you order and you can use this price for the products you sell. To ensure you have a competitive edge you want to have a discount on the MSRP which will make your product price appealing and profitable.

How to Choose a Strategy

- Make your price appealing to compensate for longer shipping times. As a dropshipper, it is hard to guarantee or offer next day shipping and in some cases, it can take weeks for products to arrive to the buyer. You can add in the shipping cost to your selling price and offer free shipping to buyers which they will perceive as a good deal.

- See if you can find suppliers that have your products at no shipping costs. Not only will this allow you to lower your selling price but, by eliminating this cost, you can increase your profit.

- Lower-priced items will often ring in a higher volume of sales while higher-priced items typically have a lower volume. This is why many choose to use a dollar amount over a percentage amount to add to their products.

- Don't forget about any extra fees that you will need to cover. Subscription fees, shipping fees, and other smaller fees can easily be an oversight and this can bring a hit to your profits. Adding a fixed dollar addition to your products along with your markups can ensure all fees are taken care of.

- Always look at what your competitors' prices are. While you don't need to price your products the same, if you can't offer a price that is slightly below or even slightly above, then you will have to rethink your strategy. If you still find that you are not able to profit by lowering the price you will need to come up with a plan to make your product stand out from your competitors and therefore make the price appealing to buyers.

Chapter 8: Legal Matters For A Dropshipping Business

Even dropshipping business owners need to understand and be concerned with some legal matters. This is not just to protect themselves but many suppliers and manufacturers will not work with you if you are not running a legal business. Taking the time to understand and obtain all the legal paperwork needed to run your business can get your business running sooner and ensure you don't run into unwanted issues in the future.

Business Structure

You will need to decide on a business structure in order to apply to make your business a legal entity. Depending on your location the paperwork for this can take a while to go through. This is one of the first things you will want to do prior to contacting suppliers or even setting up your online store because of the long wait time. You can begin building your storefront as you wait. When all paperwork has been cleared, you will receive a formal Certificate. Each state also refers to this by different names, such as a Certificate for Resale. You will need this along with your EIN to open up a business bank account.

LLC

A Limited Liability Company separates the actual business and the owner. Both are looked at as individual entities and having their own liabilities and assets. As an LLC company, you have some protection over your personal assets.

Sole Proprietorship

In a sole proprietorship, the business and the business owner are one and the same. If for any reason your dropshipping business were to be sued, then all of your assets as the owner of the business would also be business assets. Your home, car, personal business accounts and anything else that may have nothing to do with your business could be seized. While this can be the most simple business structure, there is no personal liability protection.

Requesting an EIN

EIN is an employee identification number which your business will need to acquire. In order for you to do a number of business-related actions, like filing taxes, you will need an EIN. Once you have verified that your business name is available locally you can apply for an EIN on the IRS website for free.

Local Laws and Requirements

- You must understand any restriction and clearances you will need on certain products. If you are planning to ship to multiple countries, you will have to do your research on each of these countries, as each country tends to have its own laws and regulations regarding importing and exporting goods.

- As a work from home job or home business, you will need to know if you require a business license for your dropshipping store. Some states require this and you will need to renew it regularly.

- Product Liability Insurance will help

protect you if there is any defect in the making, distribution, design, or any other danger that can occur with the products you sell. Even if you have no part or knowledge of how your product is made or who is responsible, you are at risk. Since you are a part of the chain of distribution, if there is a lawsuit against a particular product you could, unfortunately, see yourself as a defendant in these cases.

- Know about sales taxes in your area. In most states, the only time you need to collect sales tax is if your state already collects sales tax and an individual in your state has placed an order through your store. You can contact the Department of Commerce in your state to register as a retailer and learn when and how often you need to report the taxes collected.

Chapter 9: Optimizing Your Dropshipping Website

SEO stands for Search Engine Optimization and is often a neglected step when developing and maintaining websites. This refers and directly influences how visible your storefront will be in search engines. Properly optimizing your online store can help bring in more traffic and increase your ranking in search engines.

Common Things Dropshipping Websites Neglect

- Not using Google analytics. The reports you can gain from Google analytics will allow you to see what is working or not working in terms of SEO for your site. You can take advantage of the SEO reports and tactics to improve your organic reach.

- Not being mobile friendly. More and more people are searching on the go from their phones. If your website is not mobile friendly this can significantly hurt your SEO.

- Not properly researching the market. A product that isn't popular or being sought after isn't going that have good SEO even if you utilize every optimization tip and tool available. If there is no demand for that product no one is searching for it and will struggle to get traffic from search engine results.

- Not optimizing your URLs. You want your URLs to include targeted keywords and be descriptive. Along with the URLs, you can't forget about title tags and meta-description that show up on search engine results as a brief summary with the link to your store.

SEO for Dropshipping Products

How can you improve your SEO? Aside from inserting keywords into your product description and ensuring every aspect of your website is optimized to the fullest, you want to come up with a content strategy. The best way to drive more organic traffic to your site is from other sources. Blog posts, guest blog posts, link sharing that is relevant in the comment sections, email marketing, and social media posts can all drive traffic to your store. Just be aware you don't want to go out spamming every post and comment section you come across as this severely drops your SEO.

Perform keyword searches to know which keywords will be the best fit for your content. This can be easily done using Google Keywords Search. Understand how to optimize your content so the keywords show up naturally and evenly through your content. Not only will this improve your SEO by creating content, you are strengthening your brand and creating an online presence.

A final tip regarding your Shopify account, SEO Site Audit, Benchmark Hero is a Shopify app that provides you with an analysis of what is and is not working in regards to your websites SEO performance. You will be able to understand what pages are converting to sales and why others aren't. Additionally, you will be able to see what changes you should make and how your store compares to others.

Chapter 10: How to Develop Your Brand in 2019

Your brand identity is what will make your business more memorable and help you stand out to become an established Dropshipper. One of the mistakes new business owners make is not putting enough thought or time into developing a strong brand. Without a unique brand, buyers won't feel compelled to buy from you over one of your competitors.

Why Branding is Important

Your brand is ultimately the personality of your business. It can help bring in and retain loyal customers. Your brand is also what will be the cohesive traits that will be present in all your marketing, design and content strategies. The main reason you should focus on building a brand include:

- Builds loyalty. Customers are more willing to buy from a business they trust. They are also more willing to recommend brands that they trust. Without a clear brand identity that allows these customers to remember where they made their purchase from, they won't know where to return to or send others to.

- Makes you stand out. If you have done your research and looked at other dropshipper sites you will notice the ones that haven't developed a brand are the ones not doing as well as those that have. Branding can give you a major competitive edge. Your logo, language and what you provide your customers are all aspects of your identity you want your audience to remember.

- Shows what you stand for. In many cases, people are not just buying from anyone anymore. They are actively looking for a place to purchase from that also aligns with their own values and morals. When your brand can portray these aspects you can convert more of your audience to life-long customers.

Developing Your Brand

How can you develop and strengthen your brand? There are many ways you can solidify your brand identity both internally and externally.

Mission statement

When you think of some of the best-known companies, one of the things that often stands out most are their catchy phrases like

"Just do it". These phrases often stem from the mission statement of that company. Your mission statement should be a brief summary of what your goal is. What is your ultimate goal when it comes to the customer experience? Is it to provide something, be a leader in the industry, or to provide a certain customer experience? Your mission should be focused on what your customer will gain out of choosing you and the whole reason why you do what you do.

Build an online presence

Your business will thrive not just on products, but on content. Building a blog page and setting up social media accounts are not just other ways to get eyes on your store. These additional platforms can greatly strengthen your brand identity while also making your store and products stand out from competitors. Creating content around your products, target audience, and customer reviews are one of the fastest ways to gain credibility. Go back to your initial list and notes when you were first considering your dropshipping business and start to gather ideas for blog posts and topics to share on social media. Additionally, many sites can be synced up to your Shopify account so you can easily drive traffic from your blog to your shop.

Some suppliers can help brand the products they ship for you. Instead of just shipping the product in a standard box they can include marketing materials like flyers or stickers to the product packaging to help your brand stand out from other dropshippers.

Chapter 11: Email Marketing Strategies

Email marketing is not the most talked about method to grow your business. While it may be an overlooked way to market your dropshipping store, when done successfully you can see an increase in conversion rates. Email marketing will take a little bit of planning to ensure your emails are being looked at and patience as you grow your email list.

How to Create an Email Marketing Campaign

You want to have an email marketing strategy that will allow you to consistently send out newsletters to your list. The first newsletter should be a personalized welcome email that is sent to everyone you add to your email list. After the initial welcome email, the content you create for your newsletter can vary. Some ideas include:

- Focus on a number of aspects related to the products you offer, your niche, and exclusive offers.

- Create a campaign around other content that you have created such as blog post or podcasts.

- Share when you add new items to your store or have a sale.

- Send a newsletter when you have a special offer or promotion going on and add options that allow your readers to share the offer to friends and family.

- Think of a way that you can make those on your email list feel as if they are getting something that not everyone has access to like offering a discount on a certain item each week. Those on your email list are the only ones that will get the discount offer.

- Send out birthday newsletters, or a newsletter that gives a special offer to individuals based on their previous purchases or browsing history.

Use language that your audience will relate to and understand. This is why, when choosing your niche it is ideal to have a little experience or understanding about the products. The language may change as your business grows and you begin to understand your audience's likes and dislikes more.

Entice your recipients to open the email. Emails get quickly skimmed past or just deleted without ever getting opened. If you want to increase the possibility of converting your email lists to actual customers you need to have catchy headlines that grab their attention. Personalizing headlines with the recipient name can also increase the likelihood that they will open it.

Shopify provides users with a number of different apps, both free and paid, that can help automate your email campaign. This can help make starting out easier and allow you to better understand what works and doesn't work with your audience.

Grow Your Email List

To run a successful email marketing campaign you need to have an email list to send to. The most common way for businesses to grow their email list is through funnels. Funnels are a way to attract your audience in creative and catchy ways to get them to sign up to your email. These funnels can be incorporated on your storefront, blog, website, or social media platforms. They can range from quizzes that will offer recommendations for the perfect products for them, to offers for downloadable and printable material like eBooks, to templates, and how-to guides, which are the most used funnels. Giveaways and contests can help grow your list even faster as a funnel system.

Another option could be opt-in forms. You can set up opt-in forms on your website or blog that gives visitors the opportunity to sign up for your newsletters when they choose. You will want to have an appealing offer and reminder to get them to actually sign up.

You will want to have a system that can help filter and organize your email list. This will allow you to send specific marketing information to those who are more likely to be interested in it.

Pros and Cons of Email Marketing

Pros:

- Low cost of setting up and maintaining your email newsletter.

- Easily track which campaigns are working and who is opening the emails.

- Little time commitment but can reach hundreds to thousands in a matter of minutes.

Cons:

- It is not a reliable way to market, as many people never open the newsletters.

- Can take a long time to build up a sizeable email list.

- Poorly planned out email marketing campaigns can result in getting a bad reputation for spamming.

Chapter 12: Facebook Advertising for Dropshipping Business

Facebook is just one of the social media platforms that you can utilize to market and run ads on. With billions of users, you have an opportunity to reach millions of new customers or enter into a new audience. Advertising on Facebook can be complex and has its own set of benefits and disadvantages.

What to Understand About Facebook Ads

1. creative with your wording using phrases such as:

    "Do you know someone who needs one of these?"

    "Who would you buy this for?"

"This (insert product) is so cute/awesome. What do you think?"

"How would you rate these/this (insert product) on a scale of 1-5?

"Who needs this in their home?"

You are asking viewers to respond without telling them to leave a comment. The more engagement you have the more people who will see your ad, plus more engagement can lead to a reduced ad price.

2. Create a scroll stopping ad that is simple and to the point. Most successful Facebook ads display a clear image, usually just of one product, and include little content. These types of ads tend to blend into timelines which is

why they do well, especially with engagement because people don't realize it's an add until after they click or comment on it.

3. Your ad needs to be mobile friendly since nearly everyone on Facebook accesses it primarily from their smartphones.

Your total daily ad budget using Facebook should not be more than the profit margin for the product you are running the ad for. So if you have a profit margin of $20 your total daily ad budget for that product should only be $20.

Testing Your Facebook Ads

Create a tracking system that will allow you to better organize and improve the ads you run. Keeping track of the ads you are testing out will help you quickly see what parts of your ad are working and what you might need to change up.

Are you reaching the right target market? Once you test out some ads and have a few that are successful then this ad campaign is one you will want to duplicate and run for other products. Remember, just because one product does well doesn't mean they all will, but certain types of products may do very well on the same campaign layout.

Don't rule out worldwide buyers. Facebook ads allow you to target certain countries, the most popular being Australia, Canada, the US, and the UK. Often times your best customer will come from places you've never heard of. When you don't see your ads bringing in much return, you want to consider creating a worldwide ad and see what happens.

Pros and Cons of Facebook Ads

Pros:

- When you run a successful ad you can expect more traffic and higher returns on your investment.

- Ads can more specifically target the audience you want to market to and introduce your brand into untapped markets.

- Running a single Facebook Ad instead of using other digital marketing outlets can be cheaper.

Cons:

- While one ad may not be expensive, you will need to run multiple ads to see which products, styles, and audience bring in the most conversions. This can quickly add up to a major expense.

- Lower cost ads will only reach a lower range marketplace where users are not likely to buy.

- Can be more difficult to set up and get approved.

- Requires very careful planning and strategizing.

- Not the easiest to use as a beginner.

- Scaling your ads can also be a risk if you do it too quickly.

Chapter 13: Getting Started With Amazon FBA

As the world's largest online retail site you might be wondering why you wouldn't just start your dropshipping business on Amazon. While Amazon can be a great option to help grow and expand your dropshipping business, it is a bit more challenging to get into. Amazon's FBA or Fulfillment By Amazon program can allow dropshippers to tap into the massive marketplace and provides some nice perks. But, there are also some drawbacks when you decide to scale your business on Amazon.

Pros and Cons of Using Amazon FBA

Pros:

- Large audience. Amazon is one of the first places people search when shopping online. Billions of people visit daily which result is easy to access traffic to your store.

- Initial set up is easy. Amazon offers easy to follow guidelines to list your products on their site so there is no need for web hosting or additional back end processes.

- Fast shipping times. Amazon stores your inventory in their Fulfilled by Amazon warehouses and ships the products from there to the customers.

- Benefits of Prime shipping and Buy Box. These two features can help you stand out as a trusted and reliable

Amazon seller which can result in more people being willing to buy from you.

Cons:

- Not easy to scale. Unfortunately, you will not have access to customer data. This makes it difficult to build relationships with your customers and audience. Without this type of data, it can be difficult to know how you should be marketing new products.

- You cannot use certain apps like Oberlo to manage your products. Amazon has a strict Dropshipping Policy that forbids the purchasing of products from other manufacturers that will ship the product directly to the customer.

- You have to get approved before you can begin to sell with an Amazon FBA account.

Setting Up Dropshipping on Amazon FBA

Setting up a seller account with Amazon FBA is fairly simple when you already have an established Shopify Store. Start by signing up for a professional seller account using your email address-this comes at a monthly subscription cost. Fill out the additional information related to your business like business name, tax information, and address. If the products or niche you plan to sell needs approval, you will need to wait for this before you can move forward. Once approved you can add Amazon as a seller channel on your Shopify account. Once Amazon is added as a channel you can begin listing products. If you make your own products you will purchase UPC codes but most likely you will be selling products that are made by others. In this case, you will need to become a seller of the SKU for that product. Select the product and Publish to add to your Amazon listings.

If you do decide to continue to use Amazon as a dropshipping option than you will want to properly market your items and make them more attractive to your audience. Create Amazon ads to bring in more people. When you invest in Amazon ads you can be assured that your product will be seen by millions of visitors. You can also create Amazon coupons for your products. These coupons can then be listed on coupon sites to help you drive more traffic to your products. When creating your coupons be sure to consider your expenses so that when a coupon is used you still make a profit.

One of the ways you can successfully sell as a Dropshipper through the Amazon FBA program is by winning the Buy Box. This is a special feature only a few sellers can obtain but can help you sell more products and have a more organic reach in traffic to your store. To help you win the Buy Box option you will need to have a seller rating above 95%. Ensure the product will be shipped within 14 days and provide low shipping costs. Having the Buy Box can increase the chances of your product being sold over your competitors.

Useful Apps and Information:

- Do product research including keyword searches. This will allow you to see what visitors are looking for, what products are being sold most and how to properly price your products.

- When pricing products you want to be sure to accommodate for all Amazon fees.

- Know what requirements you need to meet to sell your products through Amazon.

- Consider these tools to help you ease into Dropshipping on Amazon more successfully:

    o Merchant Words- to help with keywords searches

    o Feed Check- to view all customer reviews in one place

    o Shopify- help track inventory

- Sellery- for perfecting pricing

- Feedback Express- to get more reviews and limit negative reviews

- Amazon Volume Listing Tools- to improve your selling experience

Chapter 14: Getting Started with eBay Dropshipping

Most people know eBay as an auction site to bid on various items or just to browse. People have been unloading their unwanted belongings and getting a bit of spending money in return. While famously known for auction items, sellers also have the ability to set a fixed-price on items instead of setting up a bidding time frame. As a dropshipper this allows you to choose the price you want for the products you sell. This auction site can be a place to bring in more profits, but there are some pros and cons to understand when considering this platform.

Pros and Cons of Using eBay

Pros:

- eBay can be an easy to use platform to expand your dropshipping business. Anyone can create an account and add items to sell quickly. The platform itself is self-explanatory and incredibly easy to navigate. Plus there is additional information they offer that can help post your item to see greater success.

- You'll gain a lot of exposure since there are millions of visitors a day. Many people use eBay to compare prices for items they know they want but even more, visitors land on this site just to browse. Setting up Dropshipping on eBay can give your products more exposure.

- You don't need to learn or

understand any additional tech stuff. Adding a product on the site is incredibly simple, that even with no tech knowledge you can add items within minutes.

Cons:

- There are restrictive and specific guidelines for those who wish to Dropship on their site. They are not in favor of shipping times that will take longer than a day or two. One main infringement to their Dropshipping guidelines is that you cannot sell an item and then buy it from a manufacturer to be shipped to the seller. You need to have the item already stocked and ready for shipment.

- They also pass all responsibility to

the seller. If there is anything wrong with the product the buyer receives then you are the one who has to handle the complaint directly.

- eBay is an especially competitive site for selling. Since it is an auction site, there is a good chance that what you sell is also being sold by someone else and possibly for much less.

- You'll need to do daily check-ins and research on the products you have up for sale or plan to sell.

- While you won't need to know any extensive tech details this is because there are little ways to customize and personalize your auction items. This makes it hard to stand out among other sellers and to gain loyal customers.

- Limitations are set on all seller accounts. These limitations can include what you are allowed to sell or how many listing you are allowed when selling. As you sell more, your limitations are lowered.

Setting up Dropshipping on eBay

Even though there seem to be more disadvantages than advantages, it does not mean you cannot successfully set up a Dropshipping business on eBay but it will take more careful planning. It is not recommended that you start your Dropshipping business out on eBay. You'll want to first have a well-established relationship with a supplier. If you have started your own store on Shopify, there are plugins you can use to integrate your products to the eBay site. Once you have established a great relationship and have the understanding of your own Dropshipping store, you can begin to list on eBay. The best part is that your first 50 listings are free to post (though there is a fee you'll have to pay once you do sell an item).

What You Will Need to Begin Set Up

- You'll need a payment method such as a PayPal account, credit card or debit account. PayPal is the preferred method and is easy and free to sign up for. This is to cover the seller fees, shipping label fees, refunds, and subscription fees.

- Have clear and eye-catching images. eBay allows you to add up to 12 images of your product for free with each listing.

- The description is key to attracting more buyers. You want your description to be as specific as possible and attract customers to your items.

- Do your research on how to price your products for success.

Once you have the basics done, create an eBay account. Go to the eBay website and create an account using an email address. You have the option to create a personal account or a business account. You'll want to create a business account, in which case you'll be asked to provide your business name, type of business and business address. If you plan to just test out eBay for your Dropshipping business first you can start off with a personal account and then switch to a business account later. You will have to verify your account before selling. When your account is verified you can click on the sell your items button to create your first listing. From here you will add your product description and images. You will see a tab for advanced listing options which include:

- Bulk listings
- Adding categories
- Variations of listings (such as color or size)
- Buyer requirements

After adding all the details to your listing, you'll want to consider your selling style. You can choose auction style, where you can set a starting bid and then allow customers to place a bid on the item for a duration of time. This can either bring in more of a profit or can bring in a much lower price on the items you sell. There is also a buy it now option which allows you to set the expected price for an item. Buy it now options can also be added to an auction item.

You will then set your automatic payment method for listing fees. Then your listing is ready to be made available.

Useful Apps and Information

- eBay has an app that allows you to quickly upload and add listings to your account. This can be a convenient way to keep track of your listing and answer questions from bidders around the world.

- You can use the eBay channel on your Shopify account to sync products from Shopify to your eBay store. Currently, you do need to have either a US or Canadian account and only sell in those locations. This is also only available to Shopify accounts that are on the Lite plan or higher.

- Using an app like sYakkyofy can help you find products to sell and keep an inventory of items in a virtual warehouse for your eBay store. This can result in short shipping and processing times and help you avoid going against their Dropshipping policy.

- If you see great success with your products on eBay you might want to consider upgrading to a seller store. This option offers some discounts on fees and grants more free listing.

- A seller hub is also an option to help keep your eBay items more organized. This option also provides users with additional tools to build and grow their business through eBay.

Chapter 15: Outsourcing for Dropshipping

You started your dropshipping business to have more freedom and once your store has hit a level of success many entrepreneurs realize that the little daily to-dos and tasks to keep your store running and growing become more time-consuming. Many hesitate to outsource any business task for fear of it not being done correctly or as well as you could do them. Outsourcing, however, can help free up your time to focus on the aspects of growing your business like marketing and customer retention. It is not recommended that you start your business by outsourcing all the tasks needed to build and run your business, but to wait until you have a complete understanding of what it takes to maintain your storefront. Having this understanding will help you feel more at ease when you decide to outsource because you will know exactly the work and tasks that need to be done to keep your business growing. While you may be hesitant to outsource once you create a system and find a reliable person or company to outsource to, you won't regret it when you see the increase in profits.

What to Outsource

If outsourcing makes you nervous - as it does with many beginner business owners - start with a small task. Outsourcing smaller jobs such as writing product description or doing product research can be a great way to ease into outsourcing. The process can be highly rewarding but it will also take some trial and error to find the right individuals and put together the best team for your business. You can eventually outsource all of your business tasks but you should begin with these daily business activities:

- Product research
- New product listing images (resizing, editing, creating)
- Product descriptions
- Handling customer service
- Order fulfillment
- Bookkeeping
- Content creation
- Graphic designing
- SEO expert
- Social media management
- Storefront maintenance
- Hiring a virtual assistant

Consider which of these tasks would give

you more freedom to focus on growing your business. Even if you feel like only you know how to do a certain task, you can create training videos or information to pass along to those you hire so they can understand what you expect from them. Don't be afraid to hire a few individuals for one task and then choose the best out of the group to continue with.

How to Outsource

You don't want to just hire anyone to take over these tasks. This is your business and hiring the wrong person or under-qualified person can result in big loses, not just to your profits but also to the reputation of your brand. It is important to first have clear outlines of how you conduct your business so you can better find the right person to take over. Some task will require you to outsource to specific individuals and create your own team, while other tasks may be more beneficial to outsource the task to an outsourcing company.

To find individuals that specialize in specific tasks like content creators, graphic designers and product description writers, sign-up or search on freelancer websites. You can begin to hire and build a team of individuals who can also work together to ensure that listings are up-to-date and meet all your requirements. When using these platforms to hire individuals you want to ensure that they can communicate effectively in your language and if necessary with your customers as well. These individuals can be located all over the world so you will also need to take into consideration time zone differences that can sometimes be inconvenient to work around.

Search these sites to find freelancers:

- Upwork
- Freelancer
- Fiverr
- FreeUp
- OnlineJon.PH (for virtual assistants)

Outsourcing companies can provide you with the option to hire a whole team of individuals that will take care of a number of your tasks for you. Hiring a marketing company can be wise to take over items such as content creation, social media management, graphic design and SEO; some companies also offer website maintenance. You can also find companies that can handle all your customer service needs. These agencies can provide temporary staff members that can later grow into full-time employees.

Search these sites for agencies:

- FreeUp
- HubShout
- VirtualStaffFinder
- Growth Geeks (digital marketing and more)
- TroopSocial (social media management)

Maintain and Grow Your Business

After all the initial work and time you put into developing your Dropshipping business you will want to relax and actually enjoy all the benefits. Before you get into relaxation mode you need to know what daily, weekly, monthly and additional tasks you need to attend to so your business can continue to grow. Outsourcing allows you this freedom and flexibility but there are a few other options to consider as well

Your Shopify store may be your top Dropshipping portal. To help maintain and grow your business, consider using StoreTasker. Storetasker is a hiring platform where you can hire individuals to help you build, design and scale your dropshipping business on Shopify.

Consider additional sites to grow your business like social media stores. Facebook business pages can add products to sell on their page. Starting a Facebook business page is simple and this is one task that can be easily outsourced to an individual who has the skills and knowledge to help grow your business page organically. Instagram also offers a shop feature that you link up with your Facebook shop. Once you set up both these pages you can use the Social

Media Channels on your Shopify account to link your products to your social media sites.

Pop-up shops are a little-known technique used to help grow businesses as well. A pop-up shop allows you to interact face-to-face with customers. It also gives potential customers the opportunity to see your products in person so they know exactly what they are getting. Aside from these benefits, pop-up shops are a great way to bring in extra profits during business seasons, help unload extra or older inventory, build up your Brand presence, and test whether you want to open a physical retail space.

Conclusion

It is clear to see why dropshipping has become a fast-growing opportunity for anyone, anywhere, to become an entrepreneur. While it does involve a great deal of research and planning at first, this work can be done in a few weeks or even days. You don't have to spend months or even years weighing all the options. With a site like Shopify, you can cut back on some of the tasks, like trying to find a supplier and products on your own.

Once you have your storefront set up, it is all about maintaining and growing. You will need to find new products to add regularly, create content to push more traffic to your store, and successfully market your products. Once your store has grown to a substantial size and you realize you need to start delegating tasks, outsourcing will give you the freedom you have been working for.

Outsourcing allows you to create a truly passive income stream from your dropshipping business. When you take the time to properly come up with the expectations, outlines, and training videos or guides, hiring others to take over your business will be less stressful and frightening. You don't have to work yourself day and night to keep your dropshipping business operating and that is not why you became an entrepreneur in the first place. Once your business reaches a certain level of success it will be necessary to outsource.

Dropshipping doesn't require much in start-up cost but you will need to focus your attention on researching and marketing. Eventually, even these tasks can be outsourced to the right freelancers. With all the extra free time you have, you might just consider opening up a second dropship store.

Dropshipping

Printed in Great
Britain
by Amazon